PRESENTED TO:

_____

FROM:

_____

DATE:

_____

DEDICATION

To classroom teachers everywhere—
be encouraged, be empowered with prayer.

To my husband, Chip, and children,
Christopher and Charles, whose prayers
enable me to do what God has called me to do.

The Lord God has given me his words of wisdom
so that I may know what I should say to all these
weary ones. Morning by morning he wakens
me and opens my understanding to his will.

ISAIAH 50:4 TLB

PRAYERS FROM A TEACHER'S HEART

Vicki Caruana

Tulsa, Oklahoma

Prayers From a Teacher's Heart
ISBN 1-58919-952-9
Copyright © 2002 by Vicki Caruana

Published by RiverOak Publishing
P.O. Box 55388
Tulsa, Oklahoma 74155

CONTENTS

PROVISION – Prayers for When I'm . . .

STRENGTH – Prayers for When I'm . . .

THANKFULNESS – Prayers for When I'm . . .

WISDOM – Prayers for When I'm . . .

INTRODUCTION

Where two or more teachers are gathered . . . there is a teachers' lounge! A teachers' lounge is often a den of complaints. We weary, broken-hearted teachers look for peace but rarely find it. Why? Because we're looking in the wrong place.

In His Word God has provided the encouragement and advice that we need, and He is always available to listen to our concerns, hopes, fears, and praises. Learn to take your questions to Him before entering into the teachers' lounge. It will change your focus, and it will bring you peace.

The pages of this book are filled with everyday issues and challenges that teachers face. Each prayer is based upon a real-life situation and can easily be adapted to your particular needs.

Bask in the comfort of these prayers that were written just for you, and experience the peace that has been promised you.

I pray that this book leads you to a deeper relationship with God and that it sustains you through the inevitable ups and downs of the school year.

Strengthen me according to your word.
PSALM 119:28

Visit us on the Web at *www.encourageteachers.com* to find out more about teachers and prayer.

—*Vicki Caruana*

DIRECTION

I will bless the Lord, who hath given me counsel:
my reins also instruct me in the night seasons.
I have set the Lord always before me:
because he is at my right hand, I shall not
be moved. Therefore my heart is glad:
my flesh also shall rest in hope.

PSALMS 16: 7–9 KJV

THE SITUATION:

DECIDING WHETHER OR NOT TO QUIT

I have a choice—I can either team teach next
year and only work half time, or I can quit.
I just want more time with my little girl.

GOD'S WORD ON THE MATTER

Teach us to number our days aright,
that we may gain a heart of wisdom.

PSALM 90:12

MY PRAYER

LORD, my heart aches for my child. Our separation causes us both pain. Yet the thought of leaving my classroom makes my heart ache as well. I love my time with students, and I love using the gift that You have given me. I am torn between the world at school and the world at home.

Show me where my heart should be. Show me how to live my life in a way that pleases You. I know that You will bless me if I walk uprightly on the path that You have chosen for me. Illuminate that path, Lord. I also know that Your path is a narrow one—not many choose it. Still, You promised that Your burden is light. Grant me peace in my decision, Lord. Let me know by Your Spirit that this choice is the right one. Amen.

THE SITUATION:

Choosing a Teaching Method

I know that this unit will be difficult and that many of my students will struggle through it. The text is not the best choice for this topic. I could push through it anyway, or I could try to teach it a different way. Choosing a different way would be a lot more work for me, but there's a chance that my students will learn more if I do.

GOD'S WORD ON THE MATTER

Fathers, do not exasperate your children; instead, bring them up in the training and instruction of the Lord.

EPHESIANS 6:4

MY PRAYER

HEAVENLY FATHER, so often I think of my students as if they were my own children. In many ways I feel like their parent. My duties must therefore include training and instruction but without fear, anxiety, or frustration. I am called to provide for them, love them, bless them, correct them, pray for them, but not provoke them. In everything I must set for them an example by doing what is good.

In my teaching, help me to show integrity, seriousness, and soundness of speech. Help me to be mindful of my students' strengths and weaknesses so that I might give them what they need. Help me also to teach in a way that builds my students up and does not tear them down. Amen.

THE SITUATION:

Offered a New Position

A major corporation has
offered me the job of a lifetime.
Could I really leave teaching for this job?

GOD'S WORD ON THE MATTER

*The LORD will indeed give what is good, and
our land will yield its harvest. Righteousness goes
before him and prepares the way for his steps.*

PSALMS 85:12-13

MY PRAYER

LORD, I have followed this path for many years, and I have promised to always walk through the doors You open for me. If this new path is from You, grant me the peace that I seek in this decision. I only want to be where You want me to be. I want to go where You are working and work alongside You.

If this opportunity is supposed to be my new path, I trust that I am already equipped for it and that You have already given me what I need to do it in a way that pleases You. Help me to choose with wisdom. Lead me, Lord. Amen.

THE SITUATION:

COMMUTING A LONG DISTANCE

Is teaching at this new school worth the hour-and-a-half drive each morning and afternoon? I am starting to wonder. Does the reward outweigh the discouragement I feel each day? Maybe I should transfer to a school that is closer to my home.

GOD'S WORD ON THE MATTER

Cast all your anxiety on him because he cares for you. Be self-controlled and alert. Your enemy the devil prowls around like a roaring lion looking for someone to devour.

1 PETER 5:7-8

MY PRAYER

FATHER GOD, I often grow weary of the effort it takes to get to school each day. With the challenges that I encounter on a daily basis, a long, traffic-filled drive is the last thing I need or want. I know that once I get to school and spend time with my students, the drive doesn't seem all that important. But once I begin the drive home, all the frustrations of the day collide in my mind, and my thoughts turn to quitting or at least transferring to a school closer to home.

Grant me wisdom to make the right decision, Lord. Show me what will bring You glory. I don't want to allow the enemy to distract me from what I am called to do. Reaching and teaching children is pleasing to You. If this school is where You want me to be, please help me to find peace and joy during the drive to and from school. Amen.

THE SITUATION:

CHOOSING LITERATURE

Choosing books for my literature class
has always been a challenge. The classics
aren't always acceptable anymore.
Do I follow my own instincts or
conform to the opinions of parents?

GOD'S WORD ON THE MATTER

*"Everything is permissible for me"—
but not everything is beneficial.*

1 CORINTHIANS 6:12

MY PRAYER

LORD, I believe that what goes into the mind comes out in a life. But I also believe that Your Spirit helps us to think critically about all that goes into our minds. I want to sift what goes into the minds of my students first. I want to protect them from wrong thinking. But, I also want to make sure that they are exposed to quality literature.

Help me to know the difference. Guide me in my choices. Let me not be swayed by the voices of those who do not know You. Let whatever decision I make increase my joy of teaching and my students' love for learning. Finally, let my decision be above reproach. Amen.

THE SITUATION:

NEEDING TO PRIORITIZE

I need to learn to say no. I've taken on too
many projects. I'm in charge of too many
groups. I'm not happy, but what will people
say if I tell them I can't do it anymore?
I feel like I don't even have time to teach!

GOD'S WORD ON THE MATTER

Let us not become weary in doing good,
for at the proper time we will reap
a harvest if we do not give up.

GALATIANS 6:9

MY PRAYER

LORD GOD, it is so hard not to be overcome by the stresses of the day. My heart desires to do good to all who ask me. And You have said that each of us should look not only to our own interests, but also to the interests of others. My attitude should be the same as that of Jesus Christs. He did not grow weary in doing good. He did, however, rest and take time away from the crowds for prayer.

I want to persevere, Lord. I want to do with all my might what my hands find to do. Help me to re-evaluate my priorities and to take on only those tasks that You have called me to. Help me to drop the activities I may be doing out of pride or for selfish reasons so that I can give myself wholeheartedly to the work that You would have me do. I want to bring You glory in all that I do. Amen.

THE SITUATION:

FEELING EXHAUSTED

I teach all day, go to classes at night, prepare for the next day's teaching, and then fall asleep before my head even hits the pillow. Both my family and I wonder how long I can keep this up.

GOD'S WORD ON THE MATTER

Don't worry about anything; instead, pray about everything; tell God your needs, and don't forget to thank him for his answers. If you do this you will experience God's peace, which is far more wonderful than the human mind can understand. His peace will keep your thoughts and your hearts quiet and at rest as you trust in Christ Jesus.

PHILIPPIANS 4:6–7 TLB

MY PRAYER

FATHER IN HEAVEN, I come to You broken and weary. This road I am on has a destination, but I wonder if the cost is too high. What is most important in Your courts? I want to serve in Your kingdom with the gift that You have given me, and teaching is that gift. But, I also don't want to neglect my family or other things that You are calling me to in the process.

Show me my priorities. Show me my weaknesses. Show me, without a doubt, if I am indeed on the right path. I only want to be on the road that You have paved for me. Amen.

THE SITUATION:

PLAYING CATCH-UP

The page number I am supposed to be on in math and the skill level of many of my students do not match. Unfortunately, there is no time to reteach.

GOD'S WORD ON THE MATTER

Let the morning bring me word of your unfailing love, for I have put my trust in you. Show me the way I should go, for to you I lift up my soul.

PSALM 143:8

MY PRAYER

LORD, I feel such a sense of urgency right now. The needs of my students are so many, and the time I have with them is so short. The stakes are high, Lord, and parents' expectations are even higher. You have equipped me to do every good work. I desire to bring You glory in any and all circumstances. But how can I do that now?

You reign with wisdom, power, and love, Lord. Have mercy on Your servant, and reveal to me what I should do. You are bigger than my textbook and bigger than my students' skill levels. Glorify yourself, Lord! Make Your presence known right here, right now! Amen.

THE SITUATION:

SEEKING WISE COUNSEL

I've asked for advice from my friends, but their answers don't seem right to me. Maybe I've changed because their counsel, on which I have depended so heavily in the past, now sounds hollow. Where do I turn for advice now?

GOD'S WORD ON THE MATTER

Through thy precepts I get understanding: therefore I hate every false way. Thy word is a lamp unto my feet, and a light unto my path.

PSALMS 119:104–105 KJV

MY PRAYER

LORD, the advice I'm receiving from others right now confuses me, yet You are not the author of confusion. Their advice does not bring me peace, yet You give peace. I've learned many valuable things from my friends in the past, but I must remember that they, too, have faults and will not always have the right answers. Keep me mindful of the fact that You are the only perfect Counselor and the first one I should come to when I need advice.

I seek wisdom, Lord. Grant me the desires of my heart. You said that we don't receive because we do not ask. I ask now, in the name of Your Son, that You would make Your will clear to me. Direct my feet, O Lord. Let me not be led astray. Put me on the right path. I know that Your path is narrow, but I long to follow You and You alone. Surround me with wise counsel, and lead me by Your Word. Amen.

THE SITUATION:

DEFENDING PUBLIC EDUCATION

I'm so tired of defending
public education to everyone.

GOD'S WORD ON THE MATTER

*He said to another, "Follow Me." But he said,
"Lord, let me first go and bury my father." Jesus
said to him, "Let the dead bury their own dead,
but you go and preach the kingdom of God."*

LUKE 9:59–60 NKJV

MY PRAYER

LORD, I have been caught off guard when critics confront me with the failings of public education. Even though it is my chosen field, I am at a loss for words to explain it sometimes. There are many instances when I agree with the criticism and can offer no defense.

Help me to have the right words when I need them. Show me how to express the purpose I see in public education—the purpose that drew me to dedicate my life to it. Let my speech be seasoned with vision and excitement so that others may understand my belief that public education has great possibilities. Show me how to speak with both truthfulness and hope about my profession. Amen.

THE SITUATION:

HEARING GOSSIP ABOUT ANOTHER TEACHER

I heard a rumor today about another teacher.
It was not flattering. In fact, if it goes
unreported, it is a disaster waiting
to happen. I'd hate to be the tattletale!

GOD'S WORD ON THE MATTER

*Don't criticize and speak evil about each other,
dear brothers. If you do, you will be fighting against
God's law of loving one another, declaring it
is wrong. But your job is not to decide whether
this law is right or wrong, but to obey it.*

JAMES 4:11 TLB

MY PRAYER

MERCIFUL FATHER, I have been the object of slander on more than one occasion. I know firsthand the damage it does and the pain it causes. Help me to resist the temptation to join in this gossip and instead go to the teacher and talk to her myself. Please help me to approach her with a humble heart, and give me the words to say to her.

Help me to treat her in the same manner I would want to be treated if someone had heard gossip about me and was concerned about it. If the rumor is true, help me to minister to this teacher, and let her be open to my words. If it is false, give me the courage to stand up for her against her accusers. Either way, let Your name be glorified. Amen.

ENCOURAGEMENT

The Lord is near to all who call on him,
to all who call on him in truth. He fulfills
the desires of those who fear him,
he hears their cry and saves them.
The Lord watches over all who love him.

PSALMS 145:18–20 NIV

THE SITUATION:

FEELING INADEQUATE

Sometimes, I feel weak as a teacher and am not sure if I know my subject matter as well as I should. At times like these, I struggle with feelings of inadequacy, and I nervously approach my class full of students who expect me to know exactly what I'm doing.

GOD'S WORD ON THE MATTER

Have I not commanded you? Be strong and courageous. Do not be terrified; do not be discouraged, for the LORD your God will be with you wherever you go.

JOSHUA 1:9

MY PRAYER

FATHER IN HEAVEN, I'm thankful for the responsibility I've been given as a teacher, yet right now I feel incapable of meeting the challenges ahead of me. I don't know what to do or which way to go. Please teach me Your way, Lord.

I try to walk in confidence, but my feelings often betray me. I feel weak, inadequate, and ill-equipped. Please take these feelings and use them to show me Your power. You've said in Your Word that You choose the weak among us to show Your strength. Help me to see that my weakness is Your strength. I find assurance in the fact that my weakness causes me to lean on You.

I pray that Your glory will be revealed through my weakness. The more I depend on You, the more I will learn how to do what You've called me to do. Let Your grace fall both on me and on the students who look to me for guidance. Let them see You instead of me. Amen.

THE SITUATION:

DEALING WITH REJECTION

My idea was rejected—again! I've heard stories about supportive principals, but I don't feel like I'm interacting with one right now. Sometimes I wonder if there is any use in trying to make things better anymore. No one else seems to be interested.

GOD'S WORD ON THE MATTER

Be joyful in hope, patient in affliction, faithful in prayer.
Share with God's people who are in need.
Practice hospitality. Bless those who
persecute you; bless and do not curse.

ROMANS 12:12-14

MY PRAYER

HEAVENLY FATHER, I'm so tired of feeling like I can't do anything right. When I seek the approval of those around me, I always seem to come away with nothing. Please keep me mindful that it is only Your approval I should seek. Help me to remember that although doing the right thing is not usually popular, it pleases You and brings with it Your blessings.

Sometimes it seems as though my expertise is being wasted because it is not being acknowledged or utilized. During these times, help me to surrender my talents to You and to be patient, knowing that Your timing is always best. Help me to share with others more discouraged than I and to never grow weary in doing good. You've promised that at the proper time I will see the fruits of my labor if I do not give up. Amen.

THE SITUATION:

WRONGLY CRITICIZED

"You look just like one of the students,"
one teacher said on my first day. She
was half-joking, but it was the serious
part that shook my confidence.

GOD'S WORD ON THE MATTER

Finally, brethren, whatsoever things are true, whatsoever
things are honest, whatsoever things are just, whatsoever
things are pure, whatsoever things are lovely, whatsoever
things are of good report; if there be any virtue,
and if there be any praise, think on these things.

PHILIPPIANS 4:8 KJV

MY PRAYER

FATHER, You know that I desire to do what is right in Your eyes. Yet at times, no matter what I do, there are people I can't please. It is so hard to focus first and foremost on You when there are others around who seem to be pointing their fingers at my faults.

Help me keep blinders on as I go about my daily work to filter out criticism that isn't meant to build me up or help me overcome problems. Let those blinders help me stay focused on the things that You want me to focus on. Help me also to keep ear plugs in so that what I hear and listen to is Your Word in my thoughts. Guide my thoughts toward only Your truth. All these things will be a protection for me. When the arrows come, they will bounce right off my armor as I seek and find my confidence in You. Amen.

THE SITUATION:

HAVING PERSONAL PROBLEMS

My personal life is falling apart. How can I face my students, let alone teach them?

GOD'S WORD ON THE MATTER

O my God, I trust in You; Let me not be ashamed;
Let not my enemies triumph over me.

PSALM 25:2 NKJV

MY PRAYER

LORD, it is so difficult to hide my feelings. I want to protect my students from my emotions and not allow my personal problems to get in the way of my teaching and their learning. But when I cover my emotions, I still don't feel I'm at my personal best with my students. In this situation I want the peace that You have promised, the peace that passes all understanding. Lord, release that peace to me now.

Yet if I still experience turmoil, please cover with Your love any mistakes I might make. Let Your love for me overflow into my love for my students. Give me wisdom in knowing how much of my personal struggle to reveal to them, and allow them to see Your peace at work within me. Thank You for this time of suffering. Let it work in me patience, perseverance, and finally peace. Amen.

THE SITUATION:

DEALING WITH UNMET EXPECTATIONS

The grades were not as expected. More students than anticipated fell below grade level. It doesn't matter that our school is primarily made up of migrant workers' children. It doesn't matter that we spent more time than usual on improving their reading and writing skills. I still feel as though I've failed these children, yet I don't know what I could have done differently.

GOD'S WORD ON THE MATTER

Trust in the LORD with all thine heart; and lean not unto thine own understanding. In all thy ways acknowledge him, and he shall direct thy paths.

PROVERBS 3:5–6 KJV

MY PRAYER

LORD GOD, at times I feel utterly defeated. Sometimes it seems like no matter what I do, it's not good enough. I've tried to take care of these children the best I know how, yet they are still in need.

I surrender my ways in favor of Yours. Meet the needs of these children in Your way and in Your time. Help me rest in the fact that You have already accomplished Your will in the lives of these children. You are faithful even when I am not, Lord. I place my needs as a teacher and their needs as learners at your feet. I know that You will bring us both to where You want us to be. Thank You, God, for Your faithfulness. Amen.

THE SITUATION:

TROUBLED BY A STUDENT'S DROPPING OUT

The student I have tutored every day after school throughout the year quit today. He quit school two months before the end. He was so close—so close, yet so far.

GOD'S WORD ON THE MATTER

We also rejoice in our sufferings, because we know that suffering produces perseverance; perseverance, character; and character, hope.

ROMANS 5:3-4

MY PRAYER

LORD GOD, my heart breaks when one of my own falls through the cracks. But when one deliberately walks away, I feel helpless and frustrated. Search my heart, Lord, and my mind for any shortcoming that may have contributed to his failure. If I am in any way to blame, make it known to me so that I might correct my own failing.

My students are precious to me, as I know they are to You. Draw this student to Your side. Even as he walks away, walk with him wherever he goes. And if, by some miracle, he returns as the prodigal son, let me be there watching for him in the distance. Then I will celebrate and give You thanks for his safe return. Amen.

THE SITUATION:

SEEKING PARENTAL INVOLVEMENT

Only one parent showed up for my open-house night. I was so excited to explain my program to the parents of my learning-disabled students. I hope this isn't a pattern.

GOD'S WORD ON THE MATTER

"I have told you all this so that you will have peace of heart and mind. Here on earth you will have many trials and sorrows; but cheer up, for I have overcome the world."
JOHN 16:33 TLB

MY PRAYER

FATHER OF ABUNDANT LIFE, You know the hearts and minds of my students and their parents. You know about their struggles and concerns. You have counted every hair on their heads, and You love them more than I ever could. Help me not to be distracted by this disappointment. I have to believe that the one parent who came was the one parent who needed to be here.

Thank You for the opportunity to share Your love with this one parent. She didn't need to know about the program; she just needed to know that I would be there for her child. Remind me daily, Father, that I am not here for myself and my own glory, but to serve. Amen.

THE SITUATION:

DISAPPOINTED WITH TEACHING

I only truly get to teach during two
or three out of the six hours I have
with my elementary students.
This is not what I expected.

GOD'S WORD ON THE MATTER

I know how to live on almost nothing or with everything.
I have learned the secret of contentment in every situation,
whether it be a full stomach or hunger, plenty or want;
for I can do everything God asks me to with the help
of Christ who gives me the strength and power.

PHILIPPIANS 4:12-13 TLB

MY PRAYER

HEAVENLY FATHER, so many times I let my misconceptions about teaching prevent me from enjoying the reality of it. Teaching is not at all what I expected; yet there are still children in my charge. They deserve my best effort, even if I am disappointed.

If there is something about my current situation that I can change, empower me to do so. But grant me peace to accept the things I cannot change. Help me look for the good things about teaching rather than focusing on the negatives. You have given me the gift of teaching. I want to use it wisely for Your purposes, not my own. Help me do my very best with the time and resources I've been given. Amen.

THE SITUATION:

Unable to See the Fruit of My Labor

I have never worked so hard for anything in my entire career. The grant will fund the program for three years, but the funding won't start until next year—the year after I'm gone. I feel like it was all done for nothing. I won't even get to see it come to pass!

GOD'S WORD ON THE MATTER

A man can do nothing better than to eat and drink and find satisfaction in his work. This too, I see, is from the hand of God, for without him, who can eat or find enjoyment?

ECCLESIASTES 2:24-25

MY PRAYER

LORD, as much as I try not to be, I'm disappointed that I won't see the fruit of my labor. Help me remember why I worked so hard on this project in the first place. It wasn't for my own glory or personal satisfaction, but for Your glory and the good of my students. Those are results that will be evident whether I am here to enjoy them or not. You gave me a job to do, and I need to have joy in the fact that I did the job You prepared me for.

Even Moses did not get to enter the Promised Land after so many years of struggle and preparation. God showed him the Promised Land from afar, and he was satisfied. Lord, whether You show me the fruits of my labor or not, let me be satisfied anyway. Amen.

THE SITUATION:

UNHAPPY WITH MY POSITION

After spending two weeks in a kindergarten
class as a substitute, I realize I don't
like teaching the primary grades.

GOD'S WORD ON THE MATTER

*Serve wholeheartedly, as if you were serving the
Lord, not men, because you know that the Lord
will reward everyone for whatever good he does.*

EPHESIANS 6:7-8

MY PRAYER

FATHER, You have given me the gift of teaching. Deep down, I know that I am right where I belong—right where You want me to be at this time. Still, I dislike this position. I dread the beginning of each day and am relieved when it ends. I know that this is not the attitude You expect me to serve with.

Please either move me to a new position, or help me have an attitude of acceptance toward this position. Thank You for this opportunity to serve Your people, Lord. Let me appreciate this chance to use the gift that You have given me, no matter where I end up. Amen.

THE SITUATION:

New to a School

At first I was so excited to walk into this new position. My hopes were quickly dashed, though, as I saw the long list of phone messages from parents—parents who were upset that their children were getting a new teacher. They had already judged and sentenced me to a miserable year without ever even meeting me.

GOD'S WORD ON THE MATTER

There is only one Lawgiver and Judge, the one who is able to save and destroy. But you— who are you to judge your neighbor?

JAMES 4:12

MY PRAYER

FATHER, it hadn't occurred to me that I might face opposition from parents and others simply because I am new. Help me not to become defensive, but instead to approach their concerns with understanding. People are often scared of the unknown, and right now, that is what I am to them. Help me to be patient as I try to relieve their reservations.

Please soften their hearts toward me as well, and allow them to see me as I truly am. Help the parents to realize that we have common goals and that I, too, want the very best for their children. Give me creative ideas of ways I can get to know the parents of my students and make them feel more comfortable about my being here. Also, please help me to find a true friend among the staff, someone I can trust and confide in. Thank You for always being with me, even when I feel alone. Amen.

THE SITUATION:

DESIRING RECOGNITION FOR MY STUDENTS

One of my struggling students won
the fine-arts competition in our school,
but he didn't show up at the awards
ceremony. It would have been such
a joy to watch him accept that reward.
I'm disappointed for him—and myself.

GOD'S WORD ON THE MATTER

*That everyone may eat and drink, and find
satisfaction in all his toil—this is the gift of God.*
ECCLESIASTES 3:13

MY PRAYER

HEAVENLY FATHER, I know that gaining the praise of people is not what we should hope for. I know that the satisfaction of a job well done is enough. But I wanted everyone to see how well my student had done. I wanted them to know that he has worth. I wanted praise for him!

Now I realize that neither his worth nor mine is found in the rewards of this earth. Finding satisfaction in our work is a gift from You. Help me to remember what is really important. My student soared, and though it seems as if no one noticed, You did. You notice even a sparrow when it falls. Thank You for the opportunity to be a part of this student's life, even if no one else knew it. Amen.

THE SITUATION:

DISAPPOINTED BY COLLEAGUES

How did I end up doing all the work
for the technology committee? I am just
one of five members. While others
leave the building exactly on time,
I'm still here until well after dinner.

GOD'S WORD ON THE MATTER

The sluggard craves and gets nothing,
but the desires of the diligent are fully satisfied.
PROVERBS 13:4

MY PRAYER

FATHER ALMIGHTY, You have put me in this place at this time for this purpose. I'm feeling abandoned right now by colleagues who don't seem to want to do their part on this project. You know that I want to do what is right. You know the desires of my heart. Show me how I can do the job set before me with dignity, grace, and forgiveness for those who aren't participating.

Help me not fall into grumbling but approach my colleagues in love. Keep me mindful of the fact that I can only be accountable for myself and my own actions. Let my choices be above reproach. Let my actions be pleasing to You and to those placed in authority above me. Amen.

GUIDANCE

Trust in the Lord with all your heart
and lean not on your own understanding;
in all your ways acknowledge him,
and he will make your paths straight.

PROVERBS 3:5,6 NIV

THE SITUATION:

PREPARING FOR PARENT/TEACHER CONFERENCES

To tell the truth or not to tell the truth—
that is the question. Upcoming conferences
always make me nervous. It's always
hard to find a way to tell parents
that their child has a problem.

GOD'S WORD ON THE MATTER

*You must speak my words to them,
whether they listen or fail to listen.*

EZEKIEL 2:7

MY PRAYER

LORD, please help me to speak the truth in love to each parent I talk to. I know some of the parents won't want to hear what I have to say about their children. Let me speak with wisdom and say what is just. Help me not speak out of turn or return an angry word with an angry word. Help me know when to speak and when to be quiet during our conversations.

Help me also overlook any insults that come my way. Give me gentle words that will turn away anger. I want to always speak the truth and render sound judgment concerning my students. Do not let any unwholesome talk come out of my mouth, but only what is helpful for building up my students and meeting their needs. Amen.

THE SITUATION:

FEELING ENVIOUS

I came back from summer break, and one of my storage cabinets was missing. Later in the day, I found out that the principal had given it to a new teacher. At first I was outraged that the principal had done that without even asking me. Then I remembered my first classroom and what a sparsely furnished room it was. I wish my principal then had looked out for my needs in the same way.

GOD'S WORD ON THE MATTER

She opens her arms to the poor
and extends her hands to the needy.

PROVERBS 31:20

MY PRAYER

HEAVENLY FATHER, forgive me for acting like a spoiled child. You have provided for all of my needs. I admit to You that I have been envious at times of others who seem to receive more than I do, whether in materials, money, or prestige. I desire a heart of peace because I know that envy only brings destruction.

Cultivate in me the habit of giving, for You have said, "Give and it will be given unto you." Even when You put people in my path who seem either undesirable or unworthy, help me to obey Your command to extend kindness and to meet their needs. Amen.

THE SITUATION:

BALANCING PRIORITIES

The school's test scores were released today, and my sixth graders didn't improve as I'd hoped. After all the time spent preparing them, they still are below the state average.

GOD'S WORD ON THE MATTER

Remember this: Whoever sows sparingly will also reap sparingly, and whoever sows generously will also reap generously. Each man should give what he has decided in his heart to give, not reluctantly or under compulsion, for God loves a cheerful giver.

2 CORINTHIANS 9:6-7

MY PRAYER

LORD, it is so difficult to meet all the needs of my students, while still trying to meet the demands of my superiors. Oftentimes I don't feel like my students are getting enough of my attention. Instead, I find myself spending a great deal of time drilling them on how to take a state-mandated test. I know that they learn more from me than just the answers to a test, but finding the time to do both is challenging and frustrating.

My students deserve more, Lord. They deserve the best instruction I can provide for them. Help me manage my time in such a way that I can do what is expected but still be an engaging, encouraging, and exciting teacher. I want to light fires, not put them out. Amen.

THE SITUATION:

RECEIVING CORRECTION

The semester projects that my students turned in were poorly done. Parents have suggested that I poorly designed the project.

GOD'S WORD ON THE MATTER

He who heeds discipline shows the way to life,
but whoever ignores correction leads others astray.

PROVERBS 10:17

MY PRAYER

LORD, at first I was quite defensive that parents would put the blame of their children's poor performances on my shoulders. Then I realized that if I were at fault, even partly, I wanted to know.

Reveal to me my shortcomings, Lord. My desire is that my students will learn. Don't allow me to wallow in my pride while my students sit frustrated. Pride comes before a fall, and I don't want to fall. Bless the work of my hands so that I can bless the work of theirs. Amen.

THE SITUATION:

MAKING A DIFFICULT DECISION

I couldn't get a job close to home.
This commute is exhausting, and
I'm thinking about quitting.

GOD'S WORD ON THE MATTER

*This is what the LORD says: "Stand at the
crossroads and look; ask for the ancient paths,
ask where the good way is, and walk in it,
and you will find rest for your souls."*

JEREMIAH 6:16

MY PRAYER

LORD GOD, You are my refuge and my strength. Hold me up, Lord, as I persevere on the path that You have set before me this day. I want to bring every decision before Your throne, Lord. Do I continue on this path, or is there another?

If You make this path clear to me, then I will walk in it and have peace. That does not mean the path will be an easy one. It does not mean I will not become weary following it. But it does mean that You will walk it with me and hold me up when I stumble. Amen.

THE SITUATION:

HAVING TROUBLE CONTROLLING MY CLASS

I can't believe I lost control again today.
Will I ever be able to break
free of this habit of yelling?

GOD'S WORD ON THE MATTER

*I therefore, the prisoner in the Lord, beseech
You to walk worthily of the calling wherewith ye
were called, with all lowliness and meekness, with
longsuffering, forbearing one another in love.*

EPHESIANS 4:1-2 ASV

MY PRAYER

LORD, I cannot seem to stay calm when dealing with student behavior. I've tried every earthly way to regain control but to no avail. I submit myself before You in humble admission that I cannot do this on my own.

Help me love my students, even when they are at their most unlovable. Help me model for them the behavior that I expect. Fill me with Your Spirit and enable me to be patient, loving, and kind. Help me also overlook minor infractions and stand firm on the nonnegotiable ones. Let my students know me as a fair teacher who loves them. Amen.

THE SITUATION:

LEARNING TO LISTEN

During the parent/teacher conference, the parent did most of the talking and complaining, and I did most of the listening. But what I heard in the pauses surprised me. This parent was afraid— afraid for his child's future. Maybe that's what I really needed to hear.

GOD'S WORD ON THE MATTER

THERE IS a time for everything, and a season for every activity under heaven: . . . a time to tear and a time to mend, a time to be silent and a time to speak.

ECCLESIASTES 3:1,7

MY PRAYER

LORD, I am so used to being the one who does the talking. Teachers are like that. Sometimes I'm so busy waiting my turn to speak that I forget to listen. I often allow my tongue to fill the quiet spaces until I can no longer hear that still, quiet voice of Your Spirit.

Teach me how to be quiet. I can only have a still tongue if I have a still heart. Teach me to be still. Loving the sound of my own voice only serves myself, but loving the sound of Yours serves others. I can never truly serve my students and their parents if I don't know how to hear Your voice. Give me ears to hear, Lord! Amen.

THE SITUATION:

OFFERING SINCERE PRAISE

I've learned that saying,
"Good job," just isn't enough.

GOD'S WORD ON THE MATTER

I will give thanks to the LORD because
of his righteousness and will sing praise
to the name of the LORD Most High.

PSALM 7:17

MY PRAYER

LORD, it is so easy to get caught up in the mundane as a teacher. Even words of praise can be given without thought or consideration. My students need me to be specific, but I sometimes get lazy with my words.

When the psalmist David praises You, he does so specifically. He sings of Your righteousness. He sings of Your faithfulness. He sings of Your deliverance. Help me recognize the special attributes of each of my students, so I can sing their praises with a sincere heart. Amen.

THE SITUATION:

BUILDING UP OTHERS

I left a note in my principal's mailbox today. I figured she could use as much encouragement as any teacher or student in this school.

GOD'S WORD ON THE MATTER

Blessed are the merciful: for they shall obtain mercy. Blessed are the pure in heart: for they shall see God. Blessed are the peacemakers: for they shall be called sons of God.

MATTHEW 5:7-9 ASV

MY PRAYER

LORD, I've spent too much time waiting for someone to praise me and wasted too much energy trying to please people around me. Thank You for changing my focus and placing a new song in my heart.

My desire now is to build up others. I can do that by praising a job well done or by offering a kind word. And I can do that by living peaceably among everyone as much as possible. Please help me be sensitive to the needs of those around me and find creative ways to express my appreciation to them. Help me keep my eyes on You, Lord, and help others encourage and be encouraged. Amen.

THE SITUATION:

GIVEN CONSTRUCTIVE CRITICISM

I received a poor evaluation this semester
from my supervising teacher. It says I'm
too friendly with my students and that I
need to set better boundaries. I'm worried
that this will affect whether or not I am
offered a contract for the next year.

GOD'S WORD ON THE MATTER

*No discipline seems pleasant at the time, but painful.
Later on, however, it produces a harvest of righteousness
and peace for those who have been trained by it.*

HEBREWS 12:11

MY PRAYER

LORD, I am still inexperienced in the ways in which I should carry out this job. I let pride in my ability cloud my judgment. I thought I knew everything there was to know, but I was wrong. At first I was angry and defensive about the criticism I received, but later I realized that it was constructive and only meant to improve my skill as a teacher.

My students are worthy of my best effort. They deserve a teacher who is willing to learn how to best teach them. Thank You for sending me this message. It is a message of hope. There is room for improvement. Keep me humble, Lord. Teach me well. Amen.

THE SITUATION:

LOSING MY TEMPER

I lost my temper in class today. Not only was it in front of my students—it was also in front of two parent volunteers.

GOD'S WORD ON THE MATTER

Take note of this: Everyone should be quick to listen, slow to speak and slow to become angry, for man's anger does not bring about the righteous life that God desires.

JAMES 1:19–20

MY PRAYER

LORD, please forgive me for getting angry and losing my temper. I know that I also need to seek the forgiveness of those who received my angry words and not try to defend my actions to them. Don't let my pride get in the way of doing this.

Will I look weak in their eyes? Maybe. Will my actions encourage others to seek forgiveness in the future? Possibly. But my sole motivation must be to please You and restore my relationship with You. My anger separates us. I want to be restored to You, Lord. I confess my sin to You, Father, and I will confess it to those around me. Amen.

THE SITUATION:

WATCHING A STUDENT GO ASTRAY

One of my brightest students has changed
before my eyes. He is withdrawn,
dresses differently, and falls asleep in class;
his grades barely hover over failing.
Is it too late to save him?

GOD'S WORD ON THE MATTER

*While he was still talking to her, messengers arrived from
Jairus's home with the news that it was too late—his
daughter was dead and there was no point in Jesus'
coming now. But Jesus ignored their comments and
said to Jairus, "Don't be afraid. Just trust me."*

MARK 5:35–36 TLB

MY PRAYER

LORD, not only am I concerned about this student's grades, I also fear for his very life! He is walking a dangerous path—one that could lead to destruction. Protect him, Father. Send Your angels to surround him even as he walks away from help and those who love him.

All I can see is the change taking place on the outside of him, but You know what is going on within his heart. Please send someone into his path today in whom he can confide—someone who will minister Your love and peace to him. You can right a wrong path. I trust You to keep Your hand on this student even when I cannot. Reveal yourself to him now, and bring him close to You. Amen.

THE SITUATION:

At Odds with a New Principal

Our principal left. Her replacement
does not inspire me at all.
Maybe I should transfer.

GOD'S WORD ON THE MATTER

*Let us stop passing judgment on one another.
Instead, make up your mind not to put any
stumbling block or obstacle in your brother's way.*

ROMANS 14:13

MY PRAYER

LORD, I don't understand why You have placed this principal in authority above me, but I know I must trust Your wisdom. Help me submit to her authority and see the good aspects of her methods rather than judging her negatively because she is different from what I've grown used to.

Forgive me for judging her works so quickly; I wouldn't want her to judge mine in the same way. I do not desire to make her stumble. Help me instead to make her path clear and build her up. I do not wish to be an obstacle to her. I wish only to please You. Therefore, I must do my part in enabling her to succeed. Amen.

THE SITUATION:

ASSIGNING GRADES

I know I will get a lot of criticism for some
of the report cards this term, but some
of the students have stopped working.
Parents will complain, but what else am I
supposed to do? Should I give my students
grades they don't deserve?

GOD'S WORD ON THE MATTER

I the LORD search the heart and examine the mind,
to reward a man according to his conduct,
according to what his deeds deserve.

JEREMIAH 17:10

MY PRAYER

LORD, we are commanded to speak the truth in love. Even when I assign grades, I am choosing whether or not I will speak the truth. Let me always be truthful to each student and parent, and help me render sound judgment. Help me to be able to do what is best in each situation, so that I may be pure and blameless in Your sight.

In everything, let me set an example by doing what is good. In my teaching let me show integrity that cannot be condemned. Amen.

THE SITUATION:

STUDENT TEACHING

My internship is not going the way I expected. My supervising teacher gives me no feedback at all.

GOD'S WORD ON THE MATTER

The teaching of the wise is a fountain of life.
PROVERBS 13:14

MY PRAYER

FATHER GOD, I looked forward to learning under the guidance of a master teacher, but so far, she doesn't seem to want to teach me. I go through my days in her classroom wondering if I am doing the right things. Maybe she feels she is too busy to teach me, or maybe she is under the impression that the way things are being handled is working just fine.

Lord, please help me communicate to her my respect for her and my desire to learn. Break down any barriers between us so that we can communicate openly and honestly with each other. Give me the questions to ask to draw out her knowledge and feedback. Thank You for this opportunity to learn. Help me to make the very best of it. Amen.

PROVISION

Rejoice in the Lord always, I will say it again:
Rejoice! Do not be anxious about anything,
but in everything, by prayer and petition, with
thanksgiving, present your requests to God.
And the peace of God, which transcends all
understanding, will guard your hearts
and your minds in Christ Jesus.

PHILIPPIANS 4:4,6,7 NIV

THE SITUATION:

IN NEED OF QUIET TIME

With all the demands of each day, it's often
difficult to find much-needed alone
time to talk to God and be renewed.

GOD'S WORD ON THE MATTER

I said, "Oh, that I had the wings of a dove!
I would fly away and be at rest—I would flee far
away and stay in the desert; I would hurry to my
place of shelter, far from the tempest and storm."

PSALMS 55:6-8

MY PRAYER

LORD, I have looked and looked for a quiet place—a place where I could spend time alone with You and rest from the day's worry. I need a retreat. I need time away from the world.

I know You answer prayer, but not always in the way that I expect. Why didn't I notice sooner that You have already provided me with the time and the place for quiet. My time in the car on the way to school is my time with You. It may not be a restful place in the desert; but it is a place away from the world, and it is time with You. I can be in Your presence and be refreshed—even in my car! Amen.

THE SITUATION:

UNEXPECTEDLY BLESSED

As I rummaged through the left-behind materials of the previous teacher, I struck gold. Three boxes of copy paper were buried beneath the art supplies. That was one less thing I had to budget for this term.

GOD'S WORD ON THE MATTER

You gave abundant showers, O God;
you refreshed your weary inheritance.

PSALM 68:9

MY PRAYER

LORD, finding more than I expected or could have even hoped for was the greatest gift! Thank You for paying enough attention to my life that You know exactly what I need the moment I need it. Thank You that I can depend on Your provision and that I need never worry about lacking anything.

You supply my needs in so many unexpected ways. Sometimes You lead me to supplies in places I wouldn't have ordinarily looked. Other times when supplies are lacking, You give me creative ideas for accomplishing the same goal using things I already have. Thank You for Your faithfulness and Your generosity. I offer You my gratitude this day. Amen.

THE SITUATION:

Short on Funds

The littlest things can feel like
overwhelming disasters. I'm out of
copy paper, and it's only February!
The paper shortage means when you're out,
you're out. I have to rethink everything
I had planned for the next four months.

GOD'S WORD ON THE MATTER

*I am not saying this because I am in need, for I have
learned to be content whatever the circumstances.*

PHILIPPIANS 4:11

MY PRAYER

LORD, how difficult it is to be content when it seems so obvious that I am in need! Why is it so hard for me to rest in Your provision? Why do I measure my happiness by how much I have? I desire to provide for my students richly, yet my hands are tied. I can only offer them the most meager of gifts. It is the best I can do, and I worry that it won't be good enough.

Your Word tells us to make our requests known to You—all our requests. Give me the confidence to ask for what I need. Meet my needs as You deem fit. Help me to be content whether I have been given a large budget or a small one. You will supply my needs beyond what I could even ask. Amen.

THE SITUATION:

In Need of Supplies

The supplies I so carefully ordered last spring didn't come in on time for the first day of school. I scrambled to pull together a welcoming bulletin board and personalized name tags for the students, but that was all I could do on such short notice. My students will have to wait for their books, paper, and art supplies.

GOD'S WORD ON THE MATTER

"Look at the birds of the air; they do not sow or reap or store away in barns, and yet your heavenly Father feeds them. Are you not much more valuable than they?"

MATTHEW 6:26

MY PRAYER

LORD, sometimes it is so difficult as a teacher to distinguish between things I need and things I want for my students. I have to remember that You are my God and You have promised to supply all my needs according to Your riches in Christ Jesus. Those riches may not come as supplies and materials for my classroom; they may come instead as opportunities to teach Your ways and the truth of Your Son to my students. Help me recognize that those opportunities can often come out of adversity and out of need.

Grant me the patience to suffer long. Grant me sight that I might see the big picture as You do from Your throne. In my weakness as a teacher with very little to offer in the material sense, make me strong by Your own power. Glorify yourself, Lord! Amen.

THE SITUATION:

LACKING PLANNING TIME

Why is it that our teacher planning
days get filled up with meetings?
Now, I still don't have the time
I need to prepare for my students.

GOD'S WORD ON THE MATTER

*Be wise in the way you act toward outsiders; make the
most of every opportunity. Let your conversation
be always full of grace, seasoned with salt, so
that you may know how to answer everyone.*

COLOSSIANS 4:5–6

MY PRAYER

LORD, I am so frustrated by the constraints put upon me at school. I feel limited in what I can accomplish due to the lack of planning time. I know that my frustration has come out in inappropriate ways lately. I have complained more often than I should. Calm my spirit, Lord. Give me a sweet countenance.

I know that because of their chronic complaining, You did not let the generation of Jewish people who left their bondage in Egypt enter into the Promised Land. They wandered in the desert for forty years instead. I do not wish to wander, Lord. I want to enter into what You have promised for me.

The peace I seek will not be found in more planning time; I can only find it when I rest in Your plan for me. I trust that You will equip me to do the work You have placed before me. Forgive my complaining heart, Lord. Let me enter into Your rest. Amen.

THE SITUATION:

SUPPORTING STUDENT INITIATIVE

My eighth graders decided they wanted
to do something to beautify the school all
on their own. Now all we have to do
is convince the principal to let them.

GOD'S WORD ON THE MATTER

Hope deferred makes the heart sick,
but a longing fulfilled is a tree of life.

PROVERBS 13:12

MY PRAYER

LORD, my students desire to bring about positive change in our school. Please soften the hearts of those to whom the students must petition. Guide their words as they present their case.

Even if, in the end, the students are denied their request, help them to be content. Let their reaction, no matter what the outcome is, please You and bring glory to Your name. Amen.

THE SITUATION:

CONFRONTED IN ANGER

The parent who spoke accusing words to me
finally gave me an opportunity to respond. I
was able to speak words of kindness to her.
Suddenly, her anger was squelched, and
she smiled at me. What a wonderful
way to deal with conflict—love!

GOD'S WORD ON THE MATTER

*These things have I spoken unto you, that
my joy might remain in you, and that your
joy might be full. This is my commandment,
That ye love one another, as I have loved you.*

JOHN 15:11–12 KJV

MY PRAYER

LORD, thank You for the power of Your love. I have to admit, when someone comes to me with unkind or accusatory words, love is not usually my first reaction. But on those occasions when I allow You to have control and to shine the light of Your love through me, what a difference it makes! Expressions soften, tones lighten, and real communication is made possible.

Help me, Lord, remember and put to use the awesome power of Your love. Give me the right words when I need them, and guide my tongue as I say them. I praise You today for providing me with the ability to love. Amen.

THE SITUATION:

SPENDING TOO MUCH OF MY OWN MONEY

I'm spending too much of my
own money on my classroom.

GOD'S WORD ON THE MATTER

He who loves money shall never have enough.
The foolishness of thinking that wealth brings happiness!
The more you have, the more you spend,
right up to the limits of your income. So what is
the advantage of wealth—except perhaps to
watch it as it runs through your fingers!

ECCLESIASTES 5:10-11 TLB

MY PRAYER

LORD, the money I'm spending on my classroom is beginning to place a strain on my finances at home. It's so tempting to fall into the trap of complaining that the school doesn't provide a big enough budget, but I know this isn't pleasing to You. I cannot change the minds of those who disperse funds. I can only go to the One who disperses wisdom.

Please help me make the best use of what I have been given to work with and be grateful for it. Inspire me with new and creative ideas for using things I might normally throw away. I seek the gift of resourcefulness and give thanks to You for always providing for my needs. Amen.

STRENGTH

I love you, O Lord, my strength.
The Lord is my rock, my fortress
and my deliverer; my God is my rock,
in whom I take refuge. He is my shield and
the horn of my salvation, my stronghold.

PSALMS 18:1–3 NIV

THE SITUATION:

DEALING WITH GOSSIP

Idle gossip is killing the morale of this faculty.
What can I do to help stop it?

GOD'S WORD ON THE MATTER

He that goeth about as a tale-bearer revealeth secrets;
But he that is of a faithful spirit concealeth a matter.
PROVERBS 11:13 ASV

MY PRAYER

LORD, this school is becoming full of complainers. Teachers speak ill of one another without cause. Help me to remain faithful to Your ways. Guide my tongue to speak only the truth, and bridle it when necessary. Let me never be guilty of passing along gossip. Gossip is such an easy trap to be ensnared in; please help me guard my heart against it.

Help me behave toward those around me in a manner that is above reproach. I know that I can only be accountable for my own actions. I pray that I would be able to set a good example for my colleagues—an example of how You would have us behave toward one another. Amen.

THE SITUATION:

THE VICTIM OF VANDALISM

I couldn't believe the damage that one sixth-grader could do. My classroom was in shambles. There was spray-painted graffiti all over the walls. Everything was ruined, destroyed. The overnight violation made me once again question my choice of careers.

GOD'S WORD ON THE MATTER

This poor man cried, and the LORD heard him, and saved him out of all his troubles. The angel of the LORD encampeth round about them that fear him, and delivereth them. O taste and see that the LORD is good: blessed is the man that trusteth in him.

PSALMS 34:6-8 KJV

MY PRAYER

HEAVENLY FATHER, please remind me now of Your grace and provision. Raise me up, even though I am so discouraged. I believe that teaching at this school is where I belong, but the enemy is attacking me at every turn.

I trust You to do all that You have promised. Bless me, Lord. Protect me and strengthen me. I pray that this incident is an isolated one. Draw the student who did this to You. Amen.

THE SITUATION:

IN THE MIDST OF TURMOIL

They've locked down the school. Something terrible has happened outside these walls. How do I teach? What do I teach today?

GOD'S WORD ON THE MATTER

Guard my life and rescue me; let me not be put to shame, for I take refuge in you. May integrity and uprightness protect me, because my hope is in you.

PSALMS 25:20-21

MY PRAYER

HEAVENLY FATHER, this day has turned into one full of fear and worry. I don't know if I should let my students see my concern or continue on as if nothing has happened. Grant me the wisdom to know which is the best course.

Guard these children who are in my care. I take refuge under Your wings. Let every decision I make today reflect Your principles. I know that You are in control and Your hand protects us. Let my students be comforted by that truth as well, while they watch me guide them through this day. Amen.

THE SITUATION:

FEELING LIKE I'VE FAILED

I blew it! This field trip would have been a wonderful learning experience—if I had planned it out better. Instead we forgot our lunches, arrived an hour late, and didn't have enough buses or chaperons. I feel as though I wasted everyone's time.

GOD'S WORD ON THE MATTER

Plans fail for lack of counsel, but
with many advisers they succeed.
PROVERBS 15:22

MY PRAYER

LORD, why do I continue to think I can do it all by myself? I deceive myself into thinking that I am capable of handling everything my own way and in my own time. Then when things fall apart, I have no one to blame but myself.

But I know, Lord, that You can use even my shortcomings. You can provide where I have left gaps. Your love covers a multitude of sins; please cover mine! Then show me what I need to do to improve in this area of my teaching. Surround me with wise teachers from whom I can learn a better way. Reveal them to me, Lord. Amen.

THE SITUATION:

FACING DISASTER

Natural disasters happen to other people on the nightly news, not to us. But no one told that to the tornado last night. Our brand-new school has been completely destroyed!

GOD'S WORD ON THE MATTER

Out of the south cometh the whirlwind: and cold out of the north . . . He causeth it to come, whether for correction, or for his land, or for mercy.

JOB 37:9,13 KJV

MY PRAYER

ALMIGHTY GOD, it seems as if the worst has happened. Looking around, I see little hope on the faces of those this disaster has touched. We stand still, not knowing where to turn. I don't understand why this has happened, but I do know that You are still in control and can bring good even out of this devastating event. Maybe it will wake us up to what is really important. Maybe it will bring our community together. Maybe many people will be ministered to by the mercy of those who come to help us.

Help us not to dwell on asking why this has happened but instead to focus on seeking Your face. Help us respond in a way that pleases You and brings You glory. Amen.

THE SITUATION:

COMFORTING MY STUDENTS

The chicks in our incubator died.
I've never seen so many grief-stricken faces.

GOD'S WORD ON THE MATTER

*The steps of a good man are ordered by the
LORD: and he delighteth in his way. Though
he fall, he shall not be utterly cast down:
for the LORD upholdeth him with his hand.*

PSALMS 37:23-24 KJV

MY PRAYER

HEAVENLY FATHER, my heart breaks for my students. They did everything right, and the chicks in their care died. Their love and compassion for such small creatures brightened our classroom each day. But now their hearts are heavy and their faces turned down. I know they will recover, but right now they don't know that themselves.

Lift them up, Lord. Give them a new song in their hearts. Comfort them with Your Spirit. Use me in whatever way is necessary to bring them closer to You. Then they will realize that they can be broken-hearted without being completely broken. They will know that Your love is the only love that sustains life. Amen.

THE SITUATION:

WRONGLY ACCUSED

I have been accused of something I did not do. It is public opinion that I should be fired. How do I defend myself?

GOD'S WORD ON THE MATTER

Jehovah will not leave him in his hand, Nor condemn him when he is judged. Wait for Jehovah, and keep his way, And he will exalt thee to inherit the land.

PSALMS 37:33-34 ASV

MY PRAYER

LORD GOD, I am so afraid of what is to come. I have done nothing, yet I am accused wrongly. I am Your faithful follower. Please protect me. Let Your light shine on the truth, Lord. Let my accusers see their mistake and turn from this path.

But if they do not, help me remain faithful to what is right and not act in vengeance. My job is to walk the path that You have set before me and stay focused on You. You have promised to exalt me. You have promised to walk with me through the fire when it comes. I trust You, Lord. Amen.

THE SITUATION:

GIVING BAD NEWS

How do I tell a colleague that her child is failing? It's hard enough to tell a regular parent. But when it's a teacher's kid, well, the stakes are that much higher.

GOD'S WORD ON THE MATTER

Let your conversation be always full of grace, seasoned with salt, so that you may know how to answer everyone.

COLOSSIANS 4:6

MY PRAYER

HEAVENLY FATHER, You know the hearts of all those I encounter each day. Some days I can speak highly of their children, while other days I cannot. There are even times when keeping silent is the best thing I can do.

Help me know how to answer each parent. Guide me to always say what I mean and not cover the truth with platitudes. Let everyone who knows me have confidence in the fact that I can be trusted to always speak the truth.

When I stumble and say something wrong, soften the hearts of those who hear, so they can forgive me. Then, please help me not condemn myself too harshly, because we all stumble. Even when it is difficult to tell the truth, give me the strength to say it in love. Amen.

THE SITUATION:

FEELING FEARFUL

The emergency training that we received only made me more anxious. How would I really react if a student brought a weapon to school? Would I do the right thing at just the right time? Would I be willing to shield another from attack? How can I really keep my students safe?

GOD'S WORD ON THE MATTER

Fear not, for I have redeemed you; I have summoned you by name; you are mine. When you pass through the waters, I will be with you; and when you pass through the rivers, they will not sweep over you. When you walk through the fire, you will not be burned; the flames will not set you ablaze.

ISAIAH 43:1-2

MY PRAYER

HEAVENLY FATHER, I know that I belong to You. No one can snatch me out of Your hand. For that I am eternally grateful. I also know that trials will come into my life. Some may even threaten to destroy me. You have promised to be with me through these trials. Whether they threaten my emotional or physical well-being, You are with me.

Help me to rest in Your promise, so I won't be anxious. Help me seek Your peace even in the midst of chaos. Strengthen my faith so that I will speak Your name no matter what situation I'm in, for all the power and glory are Yours! Amen.

THE SITUATION:

DEALING WITH A BULLY

I watched as they picked on him in the halls. I stood by when they tripped him in the cafeteria. He's not the only one afraid of these bullies. But how long do I stand by and do nothing?

GOD'S WORD ON THE MATTER

You shall not show partiality in judgment; you shall hear the small as well as the great; you shall not be afraid in any man's presence, for the judgment is God's. The case that is too hard for you, bring to me, and I will hear it.

DEUTERONOMY 1:17 NKJV

MY PRAYER

LORD, we are told to stay away from student aggression and to keep ourselves safe first. But if I do that, then how do I keep these children safe? If I stand by and do nothing, am I not just as guilty as the bullies? If I turn and look away, don't I just add to the injustice?

I know what I should do, yet I fear for my own safety. Help me, Lord, to remember Your power. Remind me that the One who lives in me is greater than the one who lives in the world, and You have overcome the world! Please protect this student, and give me the courage to do and say just the right thing to take care of the situation. Amen.

THE SITUATION:

FACING DANGER

The chair came hurtling toward me.
I didn't know that someone so short
could be so strong! No one told me in
college that teaching was a contact sport.

GOD'S WORD ON THE MATTER

The LORD will protect him and preserve
his life; he will bless him in the land and
not surrender him to the desire of his foes.

PSALM 41:2

MY PRAYER

HEAVENLY FATHER, school today is so different than it was when I was younger. I never expected finding myself in danger to be a major concern when I chose teaching as my profession. Yet You have promised to preserve me when I come in and when I go out each day. Build a hedge of protection around me, Lord. Protect me from those who seek to hurt me.

Then show me what I must do to be of some help to them as well. You have said that we must love and pray for those who persecute us. I pray now for those who desire to harm me. Draw them to yourself. Make known Your love for them. Amen.

THE SITUATION:

CHALLENGED BECAUSE OF MY FAITH

Everyone in my school knows that
I believe in God and depend on Him.
There are so many that plot
against me because of this.

GOD'S WORD ON THE MATTER

When a man's ways are pleasing to the LORD,
he makes even his enemies live at peace with him.

PROVERBS 16:7

MY PRAYER

LORD, I know it is impossible to please everyone. Someone is always disappointed, no matter what I do. But now there are a few who seek to discredit me and drive me away from my position. They do not know You, Lord. But they do know that I know You, and it makes them angry.

Help me focus on being a sweet smell to those around me. Let me not be ashamed of my faith in You. Draw others to You in an obvious way, and help me to do all things in a way that pleases You. Amen.

THE SITUATION:

DEALING WITH BEHAVIORAL PROBLEMS

I have tried to redirect this student.
I have tried to reward him for good
behavior. I've even tried to bribe him to
behave. I don't know what else to do!

GOD'S WORD ON THE MATTER

*If you refuse to discipline your son, it proves
you don't love him; for if you love him,
you will be prompt to punish him.*

PROVERBS 13:24 TLB

MY PRAYER

LORD GOD, I am troubled over the behavior of this student. He pushes me to my limit. Dealing with his behavior not only takes my time, but it also takes valuable time away from my other students. I know that I've exhausted the other possible solutions and need to find an appropriate way to discipline him.

Empower me with Your Spirit to walk forward in obedience to You and discipline him in a way that is acceptable within the school in which I work. Help me to find an effective way to teach him what is and is not acceptable behavior. Soften his heart toward me so that he will be responsive to my discipline and see his need for You in the process. You have asked that we live peaceably among all as much as is possible. Help me to do that. Amen.

THE SITUATION:

FEELING OVERWHELMED

As I am nearing the end of my master's program, I am even less certain that I will finish. Teaching full-time, heading required committees, and going to school at night leaves little time for me to breathe. Everything feels urgent. Everyone and everything demand my attention. I need rest, but how?

GOD'S WORD ON THE MATTER

Take no thought, saying, What shall we eat? or, What shall we drink? or, Wherewithal shall we be clothed? . . . for your heavenly Father knoweth that ye have need of all these things. But seek ye first the kingdom of God, and his righteousness; and all these things shall be added unto you.

MATTHEW 6:31-34 KJV

MY PRAYER

ALMIGHTY GOD AND FATHER, I am so tired, but I cannot seem to find any rest. Everyone expects so much more than I think I am able to do. I spend much more time running in circles than I do sitting at Your feet. I am like Martha, but I want so much to be like Mary. Show me how to be still. Show me the measure of my days so that I might put my priorities in the right order.

You know my needs; You have promised to take care of them each and every day. Help me, that I might put my trust in Your promises. Amen.

THE SITUATION:

TEMPTED TO COMPLAIN

At first I was happy we reinstituted recess at our school. Then I realized that teachers would have to give up most of their lunch hour to supervise it. So much for a scheduled break!

GOD'S WORD ON THE MATTER

What glory is it, if, when ye be buffeted for your faults, ye shall take it patiently? but if, when ye do well, and suffer for it, ye take it patiently, this is acceptable with God.

1 PETER 2:20 KJV

MY PRAYER

HOLY GOD, my utmost desire is to do my job in a way that is pleasing to You. That means carrying out my duty in a quality manner. It also means doing so with a quality attitude. It is so easy to find things to complain about, yet I know that my complaints and grumbling grieve Your Spirit and disappoint You.

Help me do my duty with a spirit of love and acceptance. Let it be so obvious to others that I have joy that they cannot help but ask me about the source of that joy. Help me be submissive, kindhearted, and joyful in my service. I can only do this if I allow Your Spirit to work within me. I yield my own way to Yours, Lord. Amen.

THE SITUATION:

TIRED OF GRADING PAPERS

Why did I assign this report?
Now I have 150 of them to
grade and no time to do it!

GOD'S WORD ON THE MATTER

Such people we command and urge in the
Lord Jesus Christ to settle down and
earn the bread they eat. And as for you,
brothers, never tire of doing what is right.

2 THESSALONIANS 3:12-13

MY PRAYER

LORD, I am weary, yet there are students waiting on my promises. My students trust me to do what I say I will do. They know me as a fair teacher. I regret this assignment, but now I must honor my part in grading it.

Sustain me, Lord, as I push through this task. Give me a light spirit so that I might grade these papers fairly. Give me a sharp mind so that I might counsel my students wisely. Give me rest, even as I do this task. You are the sustainer, and You are my rest. Amen.

THE SITUATION:

PRESSURED INTO A DECISION

He doesn't qualify, I thought. But
they want me to admit him anyway.
If I do, I'm an accomplice to lowering
the standards and placing a student
where I don't believe he belongs. If I
don't, there definitely will be trouble.

GOD'S WORD ON THE MATTER

*A truthful witness gives honest testimony, but a
false witness tells lies. Reckless words pierce like
a sword, but the tongue of the wise brings healing.*

PROVERBS 12:17–18

MY PRAYER

FATHER, the future of a child is at stake. What I do next will contribute to his fate. Help me stand for this child and be the advocate he deserves. I know that it will cost me a great deal if I stand for him, but I believe it will cost him even more if I don't.

You can see into the hearts and minds of people. You know their intent. If the motives of those who are asking for my approval are pure and they are correct in what they are asking for, please reveal it to me so that I can give the approval with a clear conscience. But if I am correct, please give me the strength to do what is right. Help me remember that You are my source and will not let me be in need. Amen.

THE SITUATION:

IN A DANGEROUS SITUATION

I took the job in the detention center because I wanted to help these teens. Once inside, I wasn't so sure it was the smart thing to do.

GOD'S WORD ON THE MATTER

Who shall separate us from the love of Christ? Shall trouble or hardship or persecution or famine or nakedness or danger or sword? As it is written: "For your sake we face death all day long; we are considered as sheep to be slaughtered." No, in all these things we are more than conquerors through him who loved us.

ROMANS 8:35-37

MY PRAYER

LORD, I know that You have called me to this position, yet I sense that danger is near. Please send Your angels to surround Your servant. Build Your hedge of protection around me. Thwart the plans of anyone who would seek to harm me.

You have brought me to this place to share Your love and grace. I know that does not come without risk, but I also know that You are always with me and I can depend upon Your protection. Please calm my trembling and lift my head. Strengthen my voice so that I can speak Your truth with volume and confidence. Amen.

THANKFULNESS

*Let us come before him with thanksgiving and
extol him with music and song. For the Lord is
the great God, the great King above all gods.*

PSALMS 95:2-3 NIV

THE SITUATION:

Encouraged by a Former Student

I saw one of my former students working in the grocery store today. She recognized me right away. At first I was disappointed at the job she seemed to have settled on. Then she told me that if it hadn't been for me, she might not even be here today—that without me, she'd be in prison or worse. She told me that my believing in her helped her to believe in herself.

GOD'S WORD ON THE MATTER

As every man hath received the gift,
even so minister the same one to another,
as good stewards of the manifold grace of God.

1 PETER 4:10 KJV

MY PRAYER

LORD, there are so many times when it doesn't seem like my efforts make an impact. Thank You for the times when You allow me to see the fruit of my labor. I sometimes wonder where those students are who were on the wrong path. I wonder if they will make it in this world and worry that my efforts just weren't enough. It is at these very moments that You send a former student across my path with a word of encouragement. You reveal to me that it was all worth it.

Thank You for watching over my students after they leave my classroom. Continue to watch over them. Draw them to Yourself. Help me to be mindful that my belief in them is just a shadow of my belief in You. And when they recognize me after so many years, let them also recognize You. Amen.

THE SITUATION:

HAVING A GREAT DAY

Today's lesson was right on target. The class discussion was riveting, and we even ran out of time. The students were actually disappointed that class was over.

GOD'S WORD ON THE MATTER

I will praise thee, O LORD, with my whole heart;
I will shew forth all thy marvellous works.

PSALM 9:1 KJV

MY PRAYER

LORD, You have blessed me with Your loving-kindness today. It was as if You orchestrated my whole day. Your presence was obvious to me from beginning to end. The children came in happy. I was prepared. My students quickly grasped the concepts, and their behavior was stellar. I paid attention to the details. None of us wanted it to end.

Will there be a repeat performance tomorrow? I don't know, but I thank You for giving me the grace for today. Whether tomorrow is full of peace or strife doesn't matter. What happened today gave me the encouragement that I needed to approach the days ahead with confidence. Thank You for today! Amen.

THE SITUATION:

GRATEFUL FOR ENCOURAGEMENT

Sometimes it takes distance to see things clearly. Tucked behind the pages of my lesson plan book, I found a sweet thank-you note from a parent of a low-achieving child from last year. It was just what I needed right at that moment.

GOD'S WORD ON THE MATTER

As cold waters to a thirsty soul,
so is good news from a far country.
PROVERBS 25:25 KJV

MY PRAYER

HEAVENLY FATHER, once in a while You leave love notes around, waiting for me to find them. I know this gift of encouragement was really from You. I'm so glad You pay such close attention to my life that You know when I need a little inspiration.

Sometimes what I need is the smallest nudge to move forward. Other days I need the kind of confidence that only You can give. Today was one of those days. Thank You, Lord, for reminding me that I am right where I belong. I'm right where You put me. Amen.

THE SITUATION:

BLESSED WITH GIFTS

I love teaching elementary school! Parents are so appreciative, and they show it at Christmas by giving me a mountain of gifts.

GOD'S WORD ON THE MATTER

A generous man will prosper; he who refreshes others will himself be refreshed.

PROVERBS 11:25

MY PRAYER

LORD, although I traditionally receive gifts from my students during the holidays, this year they came when I needed them the most. There are so many times when I wonder if what I do really matters. The gifts show appreciation, but when a parent goes out of his or her way to write me a note of thanks, I am moved.

Even though I am grateful for the outpouring of appreciation, I must remember that it is not the yardstick I should use to measure my success. Help me to be mindful of what really matters, Lord. Help me focus on the eternal rewards and not the temporal ones. You caution us not to build up our treasures here on earth because they will all eventually pass away. And if we focus on earthly treasures, we won't be focused at all on the Heavenly ones. Keep me focused, Lord. Amen.

THE SITUATION:

TOLD I'M DOING A GOOD JOB

The note in my mailbox read, "I peeked into
your room today. You're doing a great job!"
It was from my principal.

GOD'S WORD ON THE MATTER

A man finds joy in giving an apt reply—
and how good is a timely word!

PROVERBS 15:23

MY PRAYER

LORD, You know me so well. You know just what I need and when I need it. There are many days when I feel unappreciated and alone. There are other days when I wonder why I'm still teaching. But today I received a gift—the gift of encouragement. It meant so much because it came from someone I admire.

How much more do I admire You, Lord? You are worthy of all praise and admiration. You are my ultimate authority. I realize that sometimes I don't spend much time listening for Your voice or reading Your notes in the Bible. Yet You blessed me today anyway. Maybe that note from my principal was really from You. Thank You for taking the time to peek in. Amen.

THE SITUATION:

Feeling Appreciated

It had been four years since I'd left that school. Only a few of the same teachers were there. So when I went back to visit, I expected to see only a few familiar faces. My first graders are fifth graders this year. I walked into the cafeteria, and immediately I heard, "Miss Jami, you're back!" Before I knew it, dozens of my former first graders surrounded me. I hadn't felt that loved in a long time.

GOD'S WORD ON THE MATTER

Let love and faithfulness never leave you;
bind them around your neck, write them on
the tablet of your heart. Then you will win favor
and a good name in the sight of God and man.

PROVERBS 3:3-4

MY PRAYER

FATHER, thank You for small favors—gentle reminders of Your love through the children I teach. At times it seems as if there are many frustrations in this job and few earthly rewards. But a good name is more desirable than great riches; to be esteemed is better than silver or gold.

Today I was reminded that I have many children of whom to be proud. Thank You for allowing me to have a part in their lives. I am blessed! Amen.

THE SITUATION:

WATCHING MY STUDENTS GRADUATE

Graduation day always makes me cry.
I watch those who struggled receive praise.
I watch those who had success receive
their wings. It's a beautiful sight!

GOD'S WORD ON THE MATTER

*The man who plants and the man
who waters have one purpose, and each
will be rewarded according to his own labor.*
1 CORINTHIANS 3:8

MY PRAYER

HEAVENLY FATHER, You have been faithful to watch over my students all year. Many have persevered against great odds. Many have been given a second chance. Others have received glory for their performances. But they all have the same basic need—the need for You in their lives.

I pray that somehow, during the time they were in my care, they saw You when they looked at me. Maybe I planted a seed that will make them curious about You in the future. Maybe I watered a seedling with the same love that You show me each day. Either way, bless them as they go out into Your world. Make yourself known to them during the journey of their lives. And if You choose to provide me with a glimpse into their futures, it would be such a blessing! Amen.

THE SITUATION:

BLESSED BY THE PTA

Our PTA surprised each classroom teacher with an extra two hundred dollars to spend this year! My wish list is now a thing of the past.

GOD'S WORD ON THE MATTER

Whatever is good and perfect comes to us from God, the Creator of all light, and he shines forever without change or shadow.

JAMES 1:17 TLB

MY PRAYER

MOST HOLY LORD, You are faithful to provide for all our needs. At times, You even give us more than we need—more than we could ask for. I know the PTA wrote the check, but I also know that all good things come from You. You put it on their hearts to be generous. Please bless them for their diligence and the hard work they put into making this happen.

My students benefit directly from that generosity—the PTA's generosity and Yours. Thank You for blessing Your servant and for blessing the children who will benefit from this gift. I will praise You for Your providence to all who will listen. Amen.

THE SITUATION:

WINNING A DIFFICULT STUDENT

I was kind when she was cruel and
smiled at her every frown. Now she
says I was the best teacher she ever had.

GOD'S WORD ON THE MATTER

Be patient and you will finally win,
for a soft tongue can break hard bones.
PROVERBS 25:15 TLB

MY PRAYER

LORD, stubbornness is a common trait in teachers and students. I am faced with a mirror image almost daily. Thank You for using my stubbornness in a positive way and for enabling me to help soften hard-hearted students. You have blessed me with the time to offer to a student who is hurting. Thank You for showing me through Your example how to love even the unlovable.

I am grateful to be an instrument used to live out Your will here on earth. Let those I touch go on to touch others. In that way, Your love will continue to the ends of the earth. Amen.

THE SITUATION:

GIVEN A POSITIVE EVALUATION

I read my students' evaluations of
my class with trepidation. But guess what?
They like me! They really like me!

GOD'S WORD ON THE MATTER

*I will praise the Lord no matter what happens. I will
constantly speak of his glories and grace. I will boast of
all his kindness to me. Let all who are discouraged take
heart. Let us praise the Lord together, and exalt his name.*

PSALMS 34:1–3 TLB

MY PRAYER

LORD, I have been redeemed! In the eyes of students and parents alike, I am saved. They see me for what I am—Your child. You have done it, Lord. You have made straight the crooked way. You have allowed me to let Your light shine before people. You have taken a humble servant and given me influence.

I praise You for Your grace. I will shout of Your goodness to me. Let me be an encouragement to all those teachers who are disheartened. Then together we can praise Your name forever! Amen.

THE SITUATION:

BLESSED WITH VOLUNTEERS

I looked at the volunteer sign-up
sheet in amazement. Every need was
accounted for! I wouldn't have to twist
anyone's arm this year to help out.

GOD'S WORD ON THE MATTER

*We then that are strong ought to bear the infirmities of
the weak, and not to please ourselves. Let every one
of us please his neighbour for his good to edification.*
ROMANS 15:1-2 KJV

MY PRAYER

LOVING FATHER, You always provide for our needs, but it is so glorious when You provide in abundance. Thank You for surprising me with more than I expected. Thank You for taking my needs into account and then blessing me beyond them.

Help me nurture these new relationships with parents who have volunteered their time and energy. I want to encourage them and support them as they also support me. I know that You are the One who meets all our needs, Lord. Amen.

THE SITUATION:

SURROUNDED WITH FRIENDS

Opportunities for new friendships are all
around me, yet sometimes I have to look
past my own pride to see them. I recently
befriended the school custodian. I look
forward to our chats after classes
when he comes to clean my room.

GOD'S WORD ON THE MATTER

Each of us should please his neighbor
for his good, to build him up.

ROMANS 15:2

MY PRAYER

HEAVENLY FATHER, each day You put someone in my path to love. It's not just an accident or the consequence of working in a school; it's part of Your plan. Sometimes in a school, there's a sort of caste situation—levels of importance. But You do not discriminate, so neither will I. "Love your neighbor" is Your most basic of commands. When I ask, "Who is my neighbor?" You put the custodian or the school secretary or the assistant principal in my path.

Help me always recognize people for who they are and not the job they hold. They are Your children and my neighbors. Help me treat every member of our school as important. Thank You for surrounding me with good friends and giving me opportunities to meet new ones. Amen.

WISDOM

*If any of you lacks wisdom, he should
ask God, who gives generously to all without
finding fault, and it will be given to him.*

JAMES 1:5 NIV

THE SITUATION:

TEMPTED TO BE UNJUST

I caught a student cheating today.
But when I turned him in, the principal
suggested that I overlook the incident.
What ever happened to honor?

GOD'S WORD ON THE MATTER

He who has clean hands and a pure heart,
who does not lift up his soul to an idol or swear
by what is false. He will receive blessing from
the LORD and vindication from God his Savior.

PSALMS 24:4-5

MY PRAYER

LORD, sometimes it is hard to distinguish between submitting to the authority that You have placed above me and doing the right thing. It is often right to choose to overlook a wrong because of grace, but some may overlook a matter simply to protect their own images.

You see everything, Lord. You know where things are hidden, and You know the motives of the heart. Shine Your light on those things which are hidden. Reveal the motives of those who seek their own glory. Help me remain pure in my motives, and protect me as I pursue the truth of the matter. Bless me with Your lovingkindness, and vindicate me when the time comes. Amen.

THE SITUATION:

CHALLENGED BY STUDENTS' LEARNING DISABILITIES

I knew that teaching learning-disabled
students would be difficult.
I just thought I'd be able to make
a bigger difference than I have.

GOD'S WORD ON THE MATTER

Be joyful in hope, patient in affliction,
faithful in prayer. Share with God's people
who are in need. Practice hospitality.

ROMANS 12:12-13

MY PRAYER

LORD, I went into teaching to make a difference in the lives of children, especially those with learning difficulties. Yet at times, I feel as if all I am doing is teaching them how to tread water instead of how to move through it with well-practiced strokes.

Help me overcome my doubts and know what I, as their teacher, am capable of. Reveal to me any weakness on my part so that I can be better equipped to teach them what they need to know. Don't let me be satisfied with anything less than Your best for them. I want them to do more than just survive; I want them to thrive! Please inspire me with new and exciting ideas to reach them. Amen.

THE SITUATION:

WORKING WITH PARENTS

It's funny how a different perspective can make everything clear. I visited one of my most troublesome students at his home. He was so at ease, so confident there. His mother told me how she looked forward to the summer as a time for rediscovering a love for learning with her kids. I want to encourage my students in this same way!

GOD'S WORD ON THE MATTER

Whether you turn to the right or to the left,
your ears will hear a voice behind you,
saying, "This is the way; walk in it."

ISAIAH 30:21

MY PRAYER

LORD, I am humbled as I realize that I alone am not able to give my students all they need and deserve. Keep me from being blinded by pride, thinking that I am the best person for the job. The love of a mother or father can never be replaced. For those with loving parents, let me only add to the parents' expertise; but for those with no parental love, let me help fill their need.

Help me know when I should stop and when I should go. Help me know my weakness in this and all areas. Only then will I become completely dependent upon You. I will remember that anything good I do, I can only do because You made me capable. I desire to inspire my students and to be always compassionate. Show me how to do that! Amen.

THE SITUATION:

Consoling a Troubled Student

A student cried in my classroom today. She broke down after school, spilling out her loneliness and defeat. She felt alone, unloved, and stupid. I wanted to say something life changing. I wanted to turn her life around that very day. But I didn't know what to say. So we sat, and I let her cry. Before leaving she said, "Thanks for letting me cry. I could never do this with anyone else." Then it was my turn to cry.

GOD'S WORD ON THE MATTER

Rejoice with those who rejoice;
mourn with those who mourn.

ROMANS 12:15

MY PRAYER

LORD, a child is hurting, and I'm sure she's not the only one. Sometimes my students' needs seem so numerous and so burdensome. I feel overwhelmed by the broken spirits of these children. How can I possibly meet all of their needs and heal their broken hearts? I feel inadequate and weak.

But I know that You've put these particular children in my life at this time. I know that Christ's power rests on me in my weakness. So now I can delight in my weakness; for when I am weak, then I am strong. Let Your glory be displayed as I console those who need consolation. Give me the wisdom to know when to speak and when to simply listen. Pour Your mercy onto Your children. Let them feel the presence of Your Spirit when they come to me for help. Amen.

THE SITUATION:

ENCOURAGING OTHERS

It took one extra phone call per day to make a world of difference in my classroom. Making positive phone calls to parents is powerful!

GOD'S WORD ON THE MATTER

A trustworthy envoy brings healing.

PROVERBS 13:17

MY PRAYER

HEAVENLY FATHER, so often I am the bearer of bad news. Parents often cringe when they hear that I am on the other end of the phone. Thank You for revealing to me the importance of encouragement.

My desire is to be a sweet aroma to parents and their children. Let them hear Your voice when they listen to me. Let them see Your love lived out daily in my classroom. I am Your messenger of hope, of forgiveness, and of faith. Grant me the wisdom to always choose the right words to say at just the right time. Amen.

THE SITUATION:

Teaching Gifted Children

I thought teaching gifted children
would be easy. I was wrong!

GOD'S WORD ON THE MATTER

The LORD will guide you continually, And satisfy
your soul in drought, And strengthen your bones;
You shall be like a watered garden, And like
a spring of water, whose waters do not fail.
ISAIAH 58:11 NKJV

MY PRAYER

HEAVENLY FATHER, Your children demand more than I have been prepared to give. Strengthen me as I search for the right ways in which to teach them. Guide me in my choices so that I might meet their needs. When I lack knowledge of a subject, lead me to good sources of learning.

I know that I cannot meet their needs if my own have not been met. Thank You for inviting me into Your inner circle so that I might be refreshed. Let me enter into Your rest so that I might be renewed. Let me be a blessing to these students, and enable me to help them as they grow. Amen.

THE SITUATION:

FACING CONFLICT

I sat at the student-sized desk dumbfounded.
I couldn't believe another teacher
could be so mean. What she said
wasn't true. What she said was harsh.
She left me speechless. Her words stung
so badly that I had to fight back the tears.
What should my next words to her be?

GOD'S WORD ON THE MATTER

A gentle answer turns away wrath,
but a harsh word stirs up anger.
PROVERBS 15:1

MY PRAYER

LORD, right now my mouth is full of vengeance. I'm afraid if my tongue is let loose, it will destroy all my work thus far. Being quiet is not in my nature. Help me overcome my nature. Help me be still and quiet my thoughts.

Holy Spirit, choose my words and guide my tongue. Do not let fear or anger or hurt choose them for me. Instead, give me words of kindness, encouragement, and love to speak. Let no corrupt communication proceed out of my mouth, but only what will build up those who hear. Amen.

THE SITUATION:

DEALING WITH TRAGEDY

The recent shootings sparked spontaneous debate the next day among my students. Some suggested metal detectors. Others suggested video cameras throughout the school. Some suggested we pray. The discussion lasted for more than two hours. It took a great deal out of our day, but it was worth it. I learned what was inside their hearts. They learned that I was a teacher who was willing to listen.

GOD'S WORD ON THE MATTER

Before they call I will answer; while they are still speaking I will hear.

ISAIAH 65:24

MY PRAYER

LORD GOD, Your world demonstrates Your glory every day, whether in the lives of Your children or in creation itself. But there are times when the enemy's lies are quite evident and they dismay us. Give me eyes to see and ears to hear what my students need to say when they need to say it.

Help me have the sensitivity to know when my lesson plan isn't the best plan for the day—when I simply need to listen to what my students have to say. Let me be attentive and willing to teach them at all times—when they come in, when they go out, when they walk, and when they sit. Let me recognize and make the best use of teachable moments. Amen.

THE SITUATION:

CONFRONTING A COLLEAGUE

My teaching partner's style seems
to demean the students we share.
How do I tell her?

GOD'S WORD ON THE MATTER

*Some people like to make cutting remarks,
but the words of the wise soothe and heal.*

PROVERBS 12:18 TLB

MY PRAYER

LORD, it hurts me to see children humiliated. I know that it hurts You as well. I know that I must defend them, and I will. But I also desire to save my partner in the process. Will she hear my words, or will she turn from my correction?

Guide my tongue, Father. Grant me both the words and the opportunity to speak them. Soften her heart toward me so that my words will be well received. And if she does not understand my concerns, please empower me to take the steps necessary to protect Your little ones. Help me to be both bold and loving as I speak the truth. Amen.

THE SITUATION:

TEACHING SELF-DISCIPLINE

My students behaved so poorly for the substitute teacher that she said she'd never return. I pay a high price to stay home sick.

GOD'S WORD ON THE MATTER

Put them in mind to be in subjection to rulers, to authorities, to be obedient, to be ready unto every good work, to speak evil of no man, not to be contentious, to be gentle, showing all meekness toward all men.

TITUS 3:1-2 ASV

MY PRAYER

LORD, my heart is heavy, knowing that my students misbehaved in my absence. I am discouraged because I feel as though it is a reflection of my own teaching. I have imparted knowledge. I have taught them the facts. But I have not taught them some of the most important lessons.

They must learn to submit to the authorities placed above them. They must learn to be ready to do the right things. They must learn to be gentle with one another. All these things must be carefully taught. Forgive my deficiency in this duty. Enable me to do what You have called me to do in this area. Amen.

THE SITUATION:

FACING A DIFFICULT DECISION

When a child's grade is borderline, it is up to the teacher's discretion which letter grade he should receive. My decision today affects whether this student will be promoted or retained. I don't want this responsibility.

GOD'S WORD ON THE MATTER

As for you, brothers, never tire of doing what is right.
2 THESSALONIANS 3:13

MY PRAYER

HEAVENLY FATHER, I know that no matter what I decide today, someone will be disappointed. How can I make a decision about someone else's future without careful consideration? What I really need to do is give it prayerful consideration.

Clear my mind of all distractions, Lord. Make it clear to me what I should do. Reveal any error in my judgment, and grant me peace when the right decision is before me. Enable me to do the right thing no matter what the cost may be. Amen.

THE SITUATION:

FEELING STIFLED BY CURRICULUM

I don't like the writing curriculum
that we've chosen. Am I obligated
to follow it, or can I choose to use
what I think will really work?

GOD'S WORD ON THE MATTER

*Stand fast, and hold the traditions which ye have
been taught, whether by word, or our epistle.*
2 THESSALONIANS 2:15 KJV

MY PRAYER

LORD, You have created every child with a different set of needs and gifts. My desire is to teach them in a way that meets those needs and nurtures those gifts. I know that if I choose to part ways with the status quo, I may be criticized or even reprimanded. But if I continue on the path laid before me by others, my students may not learn as much as they could.

You expect me to teach to the best of my ability. Provide a way for me to make choices for my students that will bring You glory and meet their learning needs. Open the eyes of those around me, that they may be pleasantly surprised and encouraged themselves to make wise choices. Amen.

THE SITUATION:

TEACHING PROPER BEHAVIOR

Administering discipline is one of my least favorite parts of being a teacher. Still, I know that I will be cheating my students if I don't have control of the class and fail to teach them how they should behave.

GOD'S WORD ON THE MATTER

He who spares the rod hates his son,
but he who loves him is careful to discipline him.

PROVERBS 13:24

MY PRAYER

GOD ALMIGHTY, I know that the gift of teaching means much more than just imparting knowledge to young minds; it means leading children in Your ways. You are a God of order and purpose. Everything You do is carefully planned and carried out. Your will is perfect. You discipline Your children because You love them.

My desire is to obey Your precepts and commands. My greatest desire is to please You. Help me lead my students toward the truth. Help me stand firm when it is required. Let me show mercy when it is appropriate. Never let me lead my students astray by ignoring defiance or disobedience. Guide my words and my actions each day with regard to their behavior. Amen.

THE SITUATION:

PREPARING FOR HOLIDAYS

I have no idea how or if I should celebrate
the holidays in my classroom anymore.

GOD'S WORD ON THE MATTER

*Do not let anyone judge you by what you eat
or drink, or with regard to a religious festival,
a New Moon celebration or a Sabbath day.
These are a shadow of the things that were to
come; the reality, however, is found in Christ.*

COLOSSIANS 2:16-17

MY PRAYER

LORD, recent constraints on what is and is not acceptable in a public school have made decorating for the holidays almost impossible. Teachers have to be so careful not to offend anyone or to promote or exclude any race or religious group. Holidays like Christmas and Easter have always provided ideal opportunities for sharing with my students about Your Son and Your love for them, but now it's difficult to do anything at all without causing strife.

Help me know when to take a stand and when to be a peacemaker. Give me creative ideas for sharing Your love and joy without offending anyone. Most of all, help me focus on the truth of Your love in the midst of these holidays. Let all those who come into contact with me see Your love lived out in my attitude when they hear my words and when they see my actions. Amen.

THE SITUATION:

PUZZLED BY METHODS

I just realized that teaching is just as much an art as it is a craft. I had the skill part mastered, but I still couldn't see the light go on in my students' eyes. Now that the light has come on for me, maybe I can make the same happen for them.

GOD'S WORD ON THE MATTER

Blessed is the man who finds wisdom, the man who gains understanding, for she is more profitable than silver and yields better returns than gold.

PROVERBS 3:13-14

MY PRAYER

HEAVENLY FATHER, I searched for so long for the best way to teach my students. I was easily swayed by one approach or another and felt unstable in my teaching. Now I have learned that the pursuit of only knowledge and the one right way to teach is meaningless.

However, the pursuit of knowledge with wisdom brings so many blessings. Because of wisdom, I can be a teacher who is peace-loving, considerate, submissive, full of mercy and good fruit, impartial, and sincere. These are the makings of a teacher who can change lives. Thank You for showing me that good teachers aren't the results of great methods, but of great morals. Help me to be a teacher of character. Amen.

ABOUT THE AUTHOR

Vicki Caruana is a veteran educator and curriculum designer. She is author of the best-selling books *Apples & Chalkdust* and *Apples & Chalkdust 2,* along with *Success in School.*

Vicki loves to encourage teachers. She is a featured speaker at conferences for educators in public, private, and home school settings. She writes for a wide variety of publications, including *ParentLife, Focus on the Family, Parenting for High Potential,* and *Becoming Family.* Vicki is founder of Teachers In Prayer for Schools (TIPS), which creates resources to help educators bring about effective and lasting school reform through the power of prayer.

Vicki credits her inspiration to her first grade teacher, Mrs. Robinson at Mount Vernon Elementary School, who influenced her decision at age six to become a teacher, and to her family with whom she lives in Colorado Springs, Colorado.

For additional information on seminars, consulting services, to schedule speaking engagements, or to write the author, please address your correspondence to: vcaruana@aol.com or visit her web site at: www.encourageteachers.com.